A JOB vs WORK

A Practical Guide to Personal and Organisational Productivity

Frans Filipe Kandjilu

A JOB vs WORK
A Practical Guide to Personal and Organisational Productivity

Published by Frans Filipe Kandjilu
Rundu, Namibia
+264 81 331 6564
ffkandjilu@gmail.com

2 4 6 8 10 9 7 5 3 1

Layout and cover design by Boutique Books

DEDICATION

This book is dedicated to all corporate and public servants, as well as to those unsung heroes who tirelessly contribute to and positively impact their communities, even without a formal job. May your dedication and good works continue to shape and uplift our vast communities across the world. Your commitment to service is an inspiration to us all.

FOREWORD

Making a significant contribution in an organisation has long been a goal for many individuals, albeit often for the wrong reasons. In many public, corporate and private organisations, employees are often primarily motivated by remuneration rather than a genuine commitment to the organisation's goals and vision. This tendency is evident through the nature of industrial actions that have plagued many organisations in recent years, with salary increases being a significant driving force.

Frans Filipe Kandjilu poses a critical question: Are you seeking a job or work? He provides profound insights into this question in his book *A Job Vs Work,* which is a masterpiece and a must-read for young professionals and those aspiring to become great leaders poised to make a significant contribution in their organisations.

As a student of educational leadership and management, Frans has been intrigued by the lack of understanding among employees in various organisations, including educational institutions, regarding the difference between a *job* and *work*. Through his classical style of writing, Frans offers a well-conceived distinction between these two concepts and challenges the traditional view that considers a job and work as synonymous.

A Job Vs Work is not merely an exceptional piece of work by a young man rooted in a rural setting; it is a guide for professional growth for open-minded aspiring leaders in organisations marked by fluid and laissez-faire leadership.

Make sure to grab a copy, and you will never regret it!

Gilbert Likando, PhD
Associate Professor, Educational Leadership
and Management, at the University of Namibia

ACKNOWLEDGEMENTS

I express my deepest gratitude to my beloved wife, Babe Val, whose unwavering support has been the bedrock of this project. Her understanding and the space she provided during my solitary moments played a pivotal role in bringing this book to fruition.

To Professor Gilbert Likando, my inspiration since the first day I set my eyes on him in 2011 at Rundu UNAM Campus: Thank you for endorsing this book through the foreword that you have so carefully and honestly written.

I am profoundly thankful for my two sons, Valson Gabriel Kandjilu and Filson Alex Kandjilu, as well as my sister-in-law Ravel Mukwata (Pinky), whose presence and enthusiasm consistently fuel my determination to give my best.

A heartfelt acknowledgment is reserved for Alexia, the editor, and to Boutique Books, who not only served as the proofreader but also meticulously designed the layout and book cover. Their exceptional editorial work and patience were instrumental in ensuring the absence of language and grammatical errors in this book.

I extend profound gratitude to my remarkable team at CMTI. Your unwavering support has been invigorating, and I am deeply thankful for each of you being integral to our collective journey.

Mr. Augustinus Ngombe (Mr. Mind) and Kingi, I deeply appreciate your valuable contributions to this book project. Ms. Katura, your words have been a constant wellspring of inspiration, and I vividly remember your encouraging voice urging me to embark on this journey of writing books. This meticulously crafted book stands as a testament to those words, and I eagerly anticipate the creation of many more.

To my relatives and friends, your understanding and patience during times when my availability was limited mean the world to me. Your support is invaluable.

I am indebted to my colleagues at Ruben Makaranga Combined School, whose inspiration and insights laid the groundwork for the inception of this project.

Lastly, I humbly acknowledge the divine guidance of the good Lord, the Word at first, the Word with God, and the same Word that was God, whose wisdom transcends our understanding. May He continue to illuminate your paths and broaden your horizons.

INTRODUCTION

Many seek jobs, but few truly desire to work. This book aims to clarify the distinction between having a job and engaging in meaningful work, helping you enhance your personal and organisational productivity.

The term *work* is used both as a verb (I work) and as a noun (my work). This book explores the concept of *work* in both these forms. In today's world, institutions underperform, organisations fail, employees lose jobs and students face disruptions due to a lack of understanding between what is a job and what is work.

The book consists of seven chapters:

1. Explaining the difference between a job and work.
2. Highlighting the negative consequences of job-work confusion.
3. Examining why people study and what it should mean.
4. Offering ways to add value to your work.
5. Identifying workplace misplacements.
6. Advice about not relying solely on qualifications but also on your personality's strength.
7. Unpacking the reality of businesses and organisations.

Each chapter begins with questions to deepen your understanding. Summaries at the end help reinforce key points. This book is for those who aim to make a difference in their organisation or personal life by valuing their work as much as gold. By prioritising meaningful work over just having a job, you'll gain purpose and a profound understanding of both *job* and *work* concepts.

Take your time with this book, as each chapter offers valuable insights to enrich your journey. Enjoy broadening your understanding of jobs versus work and learning to recognise their significance for individuals and organisations alike.

CONTENTS

1
UNDERSTANDING THE DIFFERENCE BETWEEN A JOB AND WORK

Are you ready to explore what a job is and how its meaning differs from that of work? Good! This chapter gives you all you need to know about the two, but first please read the following questions:

- Do you believe that people genuinely mean it when they are asked, "Where are you going?" and they respond with, "I am going to work"?
- What do you perceive as the true distinction between a job and work?
- Can one work even when one does not hold a job?
- What is the real motivation behind your work, or what do people generally work for?
- Do you think that grasping the difference between what a job is and what work is can be beneficial to you?

Did the previous questions give you an idea of what to expect from this chapter? What were your answers to these questions? Let's dive in.

Work fulfils the soul and transcends the boundaries of a mere job. This implies that work, when approached as more than just a job, has the potential to enrich one's life, contribute to personal and organisational growth, and provide a sense of fulfilment that extends beyond the tasks and duties associated with typical employment.

You would likely agree with the statement that there are still people who cannot differentiate between what a job is and what work is. This confusion continues to affect the performance and productivity of individuals and various organisations and businesses. Every current or prospective committed employee or employer should prioritise understanding the difference between the two.

A job is essentially defined as a position of regular employment, wherein one usually serves an individual or a group of people. Positions such as clerk, salesperson, nurse, teacher, policeman, cleaner, security guard, secretary, bricklayer, plumber, company CEO, head of department, principal, counsellor, councillor, minister and more, fall under the category of jobs. Work, on the other hand, refers to the act of performing one's daily engagements within these various job positions, serving the people associated with those positions.

In most cases, an employee's work is defined by the job description of their particular position. In simple terms, work is what individuals in positions like clerk, salesperson, nurse, teacher, policeman, cleaner, security guard, secretary, bricklayer, plumber, company CEO, head of department, etc., do while holding their positions or job titles.

Now, a critical question arises: Do you actually perform your work, or do you simply occupy a position? Unfortunately, many people, regardless of their roles or positions, hold their titles while doing little of what is expected of them. This tendency has become prevalent even among those in executive or managerial positions, as well as those with supervisory roles. Many seem more focused on demanding respect and obedience from their subordinates, often in a commanding manner, than on supporting and facilitating the work of those under their supervision. In essence, it often seems that 'subordinates do most of the work' in many cases.

It should be logical for a junior or recently employed individual to receive the necessary support from their immediate superior. This support is meant to empower the individual, boost their confidence in the job and enhance the quality of their work. Ideally, an individual should become self-reliant and productive over time.

Regrettably, the current situation is quite the opposite. In many organisations and institutions, managers or supervisors treat their subordinates as if they were mere pawns to be mercilessly manipulated. In turn, many subordinates perceive their managers or supervisors not as supportive mentors but as adversaries, who exist solely to disrupt the working environment. In such cases, supervisors or managers are more focused on control than on empowering their subordinates with support and guidance. Subordinates often begin their days with tension and frustration, anticipating mistreatment from their supervisors or managers.

Managers and supervisors should ideally transfer their knowledge, skills and experience to their subordinates, thereby fostering growth and productivity within the organisation or institution, and benefitting the public. However, modern working environments sometimes turn into negative, competitive arenas, where everyone hinders each other's progress. This occurs when employees, employers, subordinates, managers or supervisors prioritise their job titles over the actual work they should be doing in these positions – positions that can be critical to the organisation, business and people's lives.

There is a need, therefore, for you and me to change this narrative, which has impoverished individuals, organisations and institutions to a large extent.

When the scenario is as described above, employees in different sectors will most probably be less than optimally productive.

*A **clerk*** is more likely to boast about their clerical job instead of aiming to be on top of the game in terms of keeping records, doing accounts and undertaking other routine or administrative duties.

*A **salesperson*** is expected to greet customers warmly, assist them in locating items in the store and maintain excellent communication skills, while processing purchases in a polite and helpful manner. Unfortunately, in today's reality, some salespeople can often be found in the shop or store with their hands in their pockets, displaying little or no interest in their responsibilities or the customers.

*A **nurse*** is primarily trained to care for the sick and infirm with the aim of facilitating their swift recovery. However, what we often witness in hospitals and clinics is quite the opposite of their training. It's not uncommon to observe that, upon entering a hospital, nurses appear to be occupied with tasks unrelated to patient care. They might be seen handling incomplete registers or engaged in lengthy phone calls. Unfortunately, there are documented cases of lives being lost due to the negligence of certain nurses or other healthcare practitioners.

In some instances, patients are left waiting in long queues without their condition being promptly assessed to determine the urgency of their needs. This situation can lead to delays in providing appropriate care.

*A **bank clerk*** is employed by a bank to interact with customers and handle administrative duties. However, the dream of achieving customer satisfaction remains elusive for many bank visitors today. Some bank clerks spend three to five minutes assisting a client and seven to ten minutes in seemingly aimless movements, often going back and forth from and to their desks. One might wonder whether these movements are genuinely to collect necessary items for assisting clients or simply to showcase their ability to walk in high heels (for ladies) or look smart in classic male outfits (for men). This pattern of activity persists, regardless of whether the bank is busy or not, and whether there are long or short queues of people seeking services.

If you work as a bank clerk, it's essential to value your work beyond just having a position that allows you to interact with customers. You have every right to request that your immediate supervisor provides the tools and resources necessary to enhance your efficiency in serving customers. Remind them that your primary role is to serve the bank's clients effectively.

In some cases, customers may enter the bank and unintentionally say unkind words that affect the bank clerk. You cannot control the clients' moods, but what matters most is remembering the ultimate purpose of your role as a bank clerk or similar position. Remember the adage, 'the customer is always right'? While it may not always be accurate, it underscores the importance of avoiding arguments with dissatisfied customers in public. Upholding this principle helps maintain the organisation's reputation and your own credibility. You can address any issues later, behind closed doors.

It's crucial to manage your emotions effectively and remain in control of every situation, ensuring that no client or person you serve can ruin your day at work. This principle applies not only to bankers but to employees in all professions. Professionalism should always be upheld, regardless of the circumstances. Failing to control your emotions and letting inconsiderate clients influence your behaviour can diminish your reputation and affect other clients who may require your assistance later. Angry individuals tend to let their anger dictate their subsequent actions.

Strive to be an emotionally intelligent employee rather than an average one. As Tom Alweendo (as cited in Ngombe 2021:9) reminds us, emotional intelligence involves understanding and managing our emotions, whether they be anger, fear, sadness, excitement or anxiety.

Moving forward, let's delve into aspects that are often overlooked.

A teacher is trained to be caring, loving and to accommodate all learners. Above all, they must teach, evaluate and assess the progress of each learner assigned to them. In return, they receive a monthly salary. Typically, each teacher is given a set timetable that outlines the lesson periods, which usually last for thirty to forty-five minutes each. Unfortunately, too many teachers go to school and there they sometimes laze around, failing to fulfil the duties for which they were employed.

However, there is one figure that many teachers fear: the head of the department (HOD). But why? we might wonder.

The purpose of department heads is to provide leadership, offer support and manage activities within their departments and schools as a whole. Regrettably, in many schools today, the primary focus of supervisors' discussions with their subordinate teachers revolves around lesson preparations. These preparations are inherently personal and may not have a standardised format suitable for every teacher. They are best developed by each individual teacher based on their preferred teaching approach.

One might question why an HOD would impose their own method on a teacher's lesson preparation, particularly regarding basic elements. A lesson plan serves as a guide to the sequential activities in delivering a lesson, and many such plans share common sequences. What should concern every conscientious department head most is whether their teachers have prepared something for the learners, rather than getting overly preoccupied with unnecessary details on the lesson plan.

The essence of education, and specifically teaching, lies in recognising that every learner's needs are unique, and each learns differently from the others. Similarly, individual teachers have varying teaching methods, even if they graduated in the same field and now work in the same department. Teachers could benefit significantly from their immediate supervisors if the focus shifted from lesson preparation to lesson delivery and presentation. After all, the critical point in teaching and learning is when teachers engage with learners, fostering the construction and sharing of knowledge between teacher and learner.

Remarkably, a teacher may follow the plan outlined in their lesson preparation for Class A, but the same lesson is likely to take a different course when taught in Class B. This variability is essential because education, teaching and learning are not static practices. They do not adhere to a rigid method; they depend on the classroom environment and the learners' personalities.

Given these intriguing realities, believing that a teacher's submitted lesson preparation is proof of their readiness to teach, while being unconcerned about the dynamics in a classroom and how the teacher adapts to ensure a successful lesson, might be considered cognitive dissonance.

This is a theory propounded by Frantz Fanon, which says:

> *Sometimes people hold a core belief that is very strong. When they are presented with evidence that works against that belief, the new evidence cannot be accepted. It would create a feeling that is extremely uncomfortable, called cognitive dissonance.*

All these situations occur mainly because both the subordinate worker and their supervisor often fail to comprehend the fundamental differences between their job and the work they are expected to do.

A cleaner (or an institutional worker responsible for cleaning) is employed by organisations, institutions and companies to maintain cleanliness and hygiene in the workplace. The responsibilities of this role are typically made clear in the job advertisement, during the interview, and upon appointment or assignment to the cleaning position. Nevertheless, supervisors sometimes encounter hostility and receive unwarranted complaints from cleaners, or institutional workers, regarding their cleaning duties, and this often occurs after several years of service. One may question whether these individuals were seeking a job merely to occupy a position or to genuinely engage in the cleaning work. The answer may lie in the circumstances that necessitated them to seek employment.

Similarly, **a secretary** in an organisation, institution or company is primarily employed to perform various duties, including answering calls, handling correspondence, maintaining diaries, arranging appointments, preparing reports, filing, organising meetings, managing databases and prioritising workloads. However, today's secretaries sometimes engage in disputes or arguments with their supervisors when reminded of their core responsibilities. This behaviour is concerning for those of us who wish to see individuals at the peak of their performance and productivity in their workplaces.

Now, let's turn our attention to ***company CEOs and supervisors of organizations***. How often have you experienced or heard complaints about the delay in signing or acknowledging documents? Undoubtedly, numerous times. If every document could receive immediate attention upon entering an office, services could be rendered more efficiently and effectively, reducing the delays we often encounter. Unfortunately, it seems that there is a prevailing attitude of 'I am in charge, and you will wait until I feel like assisting you.' The person 'in charge' may forget that their office exists to serve people appropriately and effectively. Nowadays, a chair with a blazer or a desk with a handbag often greets visitors to an office. Waiting for a simple signature or authorisation stamp can sometimes take a week or even a month.

Doesn't the above scenario suggest a decline in customer service that is prevalent in this era? How can we return to the basics? Indeed, there is a need to get back to the basics by understanding the distinction between a job and the actual work.

It's important to note that the description above is not meant to imply that there are no employees or employers who consistently perform their best and achieve excellence in their roles. Positive role models can be found in every workplace. We believe that there are two types of people that God presents to us: those who show us what is being done incorrectly, and those who exemplify with care and respect what they were employed to do. We should always look up to the latter individuals and commend their dedication and enthusiasm for their work.

Interestingly, it is often through these dedicated individuals that leaders, supervisors, or employers receive a sign that they should support and educate those who are not behaving properly or are carrying out activities in an inappropriate manner. Instead of looking down on or dismissing them, it's better to teach, support and encourage them, possibly through capacity-building programs and training workshops, to enhance personal and organisational productivity.

Let's also acknowledge the dedicated employees, employers, supervisors and managers with good hearts, who strive to improve employees' lives through initiatives and appropriate methods to help them achieve their goals.

Employees and subordinates who value and respect their work more than their job titles or positions are worth recognising and learning from. Those who represent the opposite should be supported and encouraged to reach their potential.

You've reached the end of the first chapter, which introduced the differences between a job and work. Have the questions posed at the beginning of this chapter been answered? Do you now have a clear understanding of the distinction between the two? Can you discuss this confidently with someone else? Good! Now, you can prepare to explore what Chapter Two has in store for you. But first, please review the summary of this chapter on the next page.

CHAPTER SUMMARY

- Failing to understand the real meaning behind the concepts of a job and of work has devastatingly affected the performance of both individuals and organisations.
- A job is usually linked to a position of employment while work is what one does in this given position of employment.
- Glorify not your job but the work you do in that job.
- Managers or supervisors should go the extra mile in supporting and empowering their subordinates, for both personal and organisational productivity.
- A healthy working environment is one in which subordinates view supervisors as support systems, and equally supervisors view themselves as responsible for their subordinates, whom they need to nurture and honour.
- You may happen to be building your empire, so give yourself wholly to your tasks when you are at work; you could remember to do so with gratitude in the future.
- Remember to embrace the notion of 'the customer is always right' and avoid clashes with impatient clients.
- 'Be intelligently emotional by not only understanding your emotions but to be able to manage them' (Tom Alweendo in Ngombe 2021:9).
- Valuing your work is the best thing you can do because your work guarantees your job.
- Serve people diligently. You were employed to work; nothing more, nothing less!
- At every place of work, you will find a person with a positive attitude. Look up to them, learn from them and grow.

- As the world changes, so does all that is found in it. Therefore, once you are found in a position of authority, do not just do the right thing, but make things right.

2
NEGATIVE EFFECTS OF CONFUSION BETWEEN A JOB AND WORK

- How does confusion between a job and work affect the institution, the company or the organisation you work for, and how does it affect your job, your work, your personal growth, your professional growth and your own reputation?
- Does the company you work for depend on you?
- Are you productive in executing your duties at work?
- Do you love your job or your work?
- Have you ever come across someone who does not seem to know how to do their work but who does know their job description well?
- What is it that really matters at work: your job or your productivity?
- What do you do for your personal and professional growth?
- Do you care about your reputation at your workplace and within society?

Just as every broken or non-functional segment in a system is worth fixing or replacing, so are individuals who are employed and yet fail to perform their duties for unjustifiable reasons. Some do not know how devastating it is to lose a job, when least expected, until it happens. Would your company, organisation or institution keep employing someone who performs below average year in and year out? The advice documented in the Bible (Mathew 7:12) affirms this: *So, in everything, do to others what you would have them do to you, for this sums up the Law and the Prophets.*

Company or organisation owners, or those in charge of personnel, grapple daily with decisions on whether or not to continue employing a certain person. Perhaps they should be informed of the fact that the person lacks the understanding of what a job is and how it differs from their work.

It is simple: view a job as an avenue through which you have an opportunity to do what is expected in order to serve people and the company or organisation. Note that what you do in a job usually involves serving either an individual, a group of people, or the organisation, institution or company, and that it all happens in unison.

How can anyone expect to keep their job if they bring almost nothing to the table? Jobs are not only to fill a space or to hold a position; they are for those who are prepared to work and serve others.

Here is some crucial information which falls under the ambit of this chapter: If you fail to draw a line linking your job to your work, you will surely deprive a company, organisation or an institution – or even yourself, if self-employed – of a golden opportunity to thrive in profitability and productivity. This is why it becomes imperative for the entities that employ people to hold onto only productive individuals. Should an employee not take such considerations into account, they are likely to lose their job, resulting in a lost opportunity for them to produce certain results at work. They could have become known in their society for the work they did; they could have become an exceptional person who was forged by their good work ethic.

Imagine being a welcoming and hardworking secretary in an institution, or a company salesperson who is really committed to their work, which is to serve those who seek their services.

Imagine being – or meeting – a teacher who puts themself in the place of their loving parents, a teacher who looks forward to seeing, meeting and teaching their learners every day.

Imagine being – or working under – a supervisor whose subordinates know they can lean on them and that they will get the necessary support at work from them.

Imagine being – or meeting – a cleaner who finds joy in doing their cleaning tasks.

Imagine meeting a bank clerk who believes attending to clients on time is productive and satisfying, who does not make clients feel as if accessing their own money – or finding anything related to their money or even services attached to their money – more difficult than the work they did to earn it.

Imagine being – or meeting – a person who triggers a happy attitude in everyone he or she encounters. One can go on and on.

Unfortunately, perhaps you have come across people who, at one point or another, have shown you the very opposite of what has been described here. Someone who has made you wish you had not met him or her, and you even end up vowing never willingly to encounter this person again.

Below is quite a practical scenario to illustrate what people often come across when visiting certain offices. A teacher by the name of Kingi (a pseudonym) narrates:

SCENARIO

There was this day, a day which I will never forget, and I hope the same doesn't happen to the person who made this a remarkably regrettable day for me. Like many other teachers, I needed to know the status of my medical aid application which, by then, had been with the HR officer for almost a month. Whenever I inquired, I was told that her supervisor had not attended to it yet.

I then became tired of going to that office, which made me resort to making calls to her office telephone. I tell you, whenever I made these calls this telephone would ring and ring, and go unanswered. It was like that until I searched for her mobile phone number, which I then got. This other day, I called the number and she immediately picked up the call. I am sure she regretted having picked it up after she heard it was me again. You could not imagine the words she directed at me.

Immediately, she asked, 'Why did you call my personal number when I have an office number through which I should be reached at work? I don't like people to reach me through my mobile number for work-related issues.'

At first, I was a bit puzzled and rather speechless, especially knowing I had got tired of calling the very office number she claimed I should have used for anything related to her work. As a critical person, however, I considered the bad things I was thinking at that moment, bad things that I was about to say to her, but I suddenly realised that she needed my help more than I needed hers.

After she hung up on me, I drove to her office. Upon arriving there, I found her seated and comfortably sorting out papers on her table. I greeted her and explained that I had been forced to drive there after she had hung up on me.

'Oh, okay!' she said. 'I have an office telephone, so why did you choose to call me on my mobile? I don't like it.'

I told her that I had called the telephone number for almost a whole day and had also been in and out of her office for nearly a month. Her response to this was, 'If a person is busy, she is busy. What did you expect me to do if I was busy? You are very impatient. What is wrong with you people? Learn to wait, even if you need something urgently.'

Fortunately, somebody else walked into her office and heard the conversation between me and the HR officer, and that I was inquiring about the status of my medical aid application, which had been with her and her supervisor for approximately a month. Out of nowhere, she said, 'I'm also tired of calling this office number and nobody ever picks up my calls.'

I then said, 'So it's not only me who got tired of this office's tardy services, um! I was employed to teach, HR officer, and because I and other teachers need things – such as having our medical aid processed – you are employed. In other words, you are in this office because teachers exist. If we did not, I wouldn't expect you to be here. You are, therefore, here to make sure that your work benefits teachers in the shortest time possible, so as to prevent teachers coming to your office because that should not be necessary. How you manage it is up to you, but the fact remains that you are obliged to attend to us, regardless of your workload incompetence. It is not your choice to decide which teacher to attend to and which not. Just as I may not choose when and which of my classes I attend to. I must attend to all of them as per my daily timetable.'

For a moment, she looked shocked and perplexed. I left her office knowing that she had learned a thing or two. Amazingly, the next day I received a call from her mobile number telling me that my application was signed and would be forwarded to the next office in the capital city for further processing. However, a proviso allows a member to forward this application personally, which is usually quicker, and the medical aid card would be ready almost immediately.

I said, 'Thank you so much. I'd like to collect it and forward it myself.'

She said, 'No problem!'

I did the necessary, forwarded the form to the city and within three days I received my card. We became very good friends. Each has the other's mobile number and, from time to time, we check up on each other.

The above personal account – a real-life narration – provides you with an insight into what can happen when someone lacks an understanding about how their job relates to and differs from their work. People say, 'There is always someone not doing their job somewhere,' but I differ and rather tend to say, 'There is always someone not doing their work somewhere'. The result of the process is that a number of innocent people suffer. According to what has just been outlined, a number of teachers suffered, and may continue to be suffering, at the hands of the HR personnel.

By the HR officer not knowing, or failing to understand, what in general her job entailed and what in particular her work was really supposed to be, people were affected. Believing whatever it was she believed gave her the reason to sit in that office, paying little attention to how to serve the teachers with the required highest diligence. As a result, she became moody at work, choosing which call to answer and which teacher to attend to, at whichever time it suited her.

Work is what you do for whomever is supposed to receive your service, whereas a job provides you with an opportunity, or an environment, to do your work wholeheartedly. Unknowingly, the HR officer affected or affects the efficiency and effectiveness of the regional office of the education ministry by doing what she does her way. If somebody decided to evaluate her work, it would most likely amount to little compared to that done by another HR officer with a different ethic, one who places value on the work within the job.

The lady who had by chance walked into the HR officer's office and found Kingi talking to her about his medical aid application – and heard that he had been waiting for nearly a month – concluded that what people said about the HR officer must be true. The lady had, herself, arrived for the same reason. This did more to tarnish the HR officer's reputation, which was, unfortunately, being weighed up and categorised further. In future, whenever the HR officer was mentioned in this lady's presence, or when the lady spoke to others about the poorly managed office, the HR officer's bad reputation would be compounded. She would be labelled as one who lazes around at her workplace and misuses the office from which she should serve the people, teachers in particular. Ultimately, if a chance ever arose of her being promoted, or if she happened to apply for a job elsewhere, her treatment of those whom she needed to serve would haunt her, and negatively affect her professional life and career.

Every person, especially an applicant, expects that panellists – whenever a judgement or job recommendation or decision is to be made – will consider them and will know every single positive thing about them: things which provide clues to their personality and to the way they are regarded, both currently and for their work ethic in previous jobs.

Therefore, building your professional profile is as important as building your personal reputation, and remember that your reputation directly influences your professional status. Our lives build on and reflect everything we do at any given moment, small and big, whether we consider the act important or not important. In the end, it is about being conscious of every act every moment, so that our personal reputations build up our professional lives for possible growth along our chosen career paths.

Note that, although you may not love your job (because certain jobs have several issues pertaining to their conditions) or your work, if you consider that your work matters the most you should, consequently, love the work that you do or intend to do. Let your work ethic reflect how passionate you are about making a difference to the company, organisation or institution you work for, or even to the society in which you find yourself.

Joy is found in the work of your precious hands, and not in the job you find yourself doing. A job may come and go, but your work will remain forever. It will be left either as physical proof of your endeavours, or it will be observed in those who have benefitted, or will benefit, from it. Think about the level of dedication that supported the urge of those who fought for the liberation of their countries.

Congratulations! You have come to the end of this chapter, and I hope you have taken in all that it has presented to you. If not, you can always go through it again, because the goal of the chapter is to provide you with an insight into what could be confusing about your job and your work. Are you ready to move on to the next chapter? I sense a powerful YES in you. In this case, familiarise yourself with Chapter Three by reading the introductory questions first.

CHAPTER SUMMARY

- Certain company owners have no alternative but to replace whatever does not function properly or does not add value to their company's cause. This means, nowadays, that non-performing individuals are likely to lose their jobs.
- If you fail to draw the lines that links a job to work, you will surely rob any company, organisation or institution – or even yourself, if self-employed – of a golden opportunity to thrive in profit or productivity.
- They say, 'There is always someone who is not doing their job somewhere,' but I beg to differ and rather say that 'There is always someone who is not doing their work somewhere.'
- At work, monitor your mood swings so that you are not carried away by the effects thereof and allowing how you feel to reflect on the way you attend to clients.
- At the end of every day, after work try to take stock of your conduct. This will help you improve and to understand your work better and respect it more.
- Your work is what an organisation depends on for its efficiency and effectiveness.
- You may not love your job (because certain jobs have issues pertaining to their conditions), or your work, but consider that your work matters the most. This should make you love the work you do or intend to do.
- Build your professional profile by valuing what you do, both personally or through a job you are hired to do.

3
INTENTIONS OF STUDYING IN RELATION TO PRODUCTIVITY

Read the following questions to get you started and give yourself a glimpse of what Chapter Three is about.

- The importance of studying cannot be overemphasised; the question is what motivates you – and people generally – to study?
- What does studying mean to you?
- Do people study for a job, to work, or simply for the knowledge acquired?
- Have you ever come across someone who completed their studies but hardly seems well qualified?
- What do you think went wrong when someone fails to display that studying has benefitted them?
- Do you believe that studying should change the way people think and do things?

Whether or not you are considering going to college or university, or whether you just want to enrol on a course to expand your knowledge, studying has a number of benefits. These range from gaining essential skills that promote enjoyment of your career, to finally figuring out which job is actually right for you.

The main purpose of this chapter is to examine possible reasons why people study. Abriel Cleaver (2016) lists forty important reasons why people should keep studying. However, for the purposes of precision and of remaining faithful to this chapter's objectives, only four of these are examined. They are: to become educated; to earn a degree; to get more money; for self-pride.

To get an education

It is important first to understand what education is. If you look it up in dictionaries, you will come across various definitions, many of which interpret it traditionally – as a method of transferring knowledge from a teacher or lecturer to a learner or student. The Action for Social Development and Environmental Protection Organisation (ASDEPO) provides some definitions of education, such as: 'Education is the socially organised and regulated process of socially transmitting significant experiences from previous to following generations', or 'Education is the transmission of civilization.'

The problem with these views about education is that they fail to answer questions such as this one: Why do teachers or educators ask learners or students to do homework if education is said to be merely the transfer of knowledge? Or: Can we examine education to consciously consider how it benefits the lives of those who receive it, the people around them and the society they live in?

Naziev *(see references)* cites Hegel's concept of education that could help in providing a logical direction. It says:

Education is an intentional process where a person, as an individual, stands in relation to him- or herself. This happens through two different aspects. The first is his or her individuality and the second is his or her universal essence. His or her duty to him- or herself consists partly in his or her duty to care for his or her physical preservation, partly in his or her duty to educate him- or herself, to elevate his or her being as an individual into conformity with his or her universal nature.

In short, Hegel's views on education suggest that it offers more than mere personal benefits. These perspectives lead us to believe that education has the power to fundamentally alter an individual's outlook on life, influencing their approaches to various aspects. Education should not only provide individuals with the means to enhance their lives but also equip them with ideas that can contribute to the betterment of organisations, institutions and society as a whole.

Therefore, the education one acquires should foster an understanding that the role or position one occupies must not obscure the purpose and significance of the work undertaken for the company, organisation, institution, the general public and oneself. Education should empower individuals to thrive in all aspects of life, including their professional endeavours, with the resultant improvement in their work. The wise words of Albert Einstein resonate well with this concept. He states, 'Education is not the learning of facts but the training of the mind to think'.

At the end of the day, the difference made comes from the personal effort you invest. This is why some individuals, who haven't had the opportunity of formal education, may be even more productive and effective in their jobs than their educated counterparts. However, despite the controversy, education undeniably remains a paramount achievement in our time.

Organisations, institutions, companies, societies, countries, and the entire world require educated individuals and independent thinkers. This need arises from the increasing complexity and susceptibility to massive changes in our world. Adaptive and creative minds are indispensable.

The disarray within organisations and institutions can often be attributed to the individuals involved in planning, managing and leading them. Similarly, many countries experience upheavals, and upon closer examination, it becomes apparent that something might be seriously amiss with the people governing them.

Let's conclude this section with the following motivational quotes:

- 'When you create a difference in someone's life, you not only impact their life but also influence everyone connected to them throughout their entire lifetime. No act is ever too small; one by one, this is how oceans rise.' (Danielle Doby)
- 'Education is one of the most powerful things in life. It allows us to find the meaning behind everything and helps improve lives in a massive way.' (W.B. Yeats)
- 'Education gives us an understanding of the world around us and offers us an opportunity to use that knowledge wisely.' (Unknown)
- 'Overall, education is the platform that makes it possible to overcome all barriers.' (Unknown)

To earn a degree

Another intentionally chosen reason why people pursue education is to obtain a degree. Few jobs seem to consider individuals unless they possess a degree or are actively working towards obtaining one. Given this reality, it becomes challenging for individuals to study for more logical, conscious and genuinely beneficial purposes.

Rarely do people decide to pursue education with the explicit intention of positively impacting the lives of those around them or becoming more productive in their current or future employment. This trend has proven costly for organisations, institutions and even entire countries. Organisations and institutions face narrow profit margins, and countries experience issues such as poor service delivery, unemployment and international debt.

A considerable number of individuals complete an entire course, spanning, for instance, four years, only to show no improvement in their skills, reasoning abilities or, most importantly, their interactions with others. It seems that some individuals pursue education solely for the purpose of obtaining a degree.

Researchers and observers have delved into these issues, concluding that pursuing a degree without a broader purpose often leads to graduates who struggle to apply their knowledge beyond the specific scope of their degrees. Hence, the aptly coined saying: 'Your degree is just a piece of paper; your behaviour should reflect the level of your education.'

To get more money

Once again, there are numerous individuals who pursue education with the primary goal of increasing their income. The notion that 'your degree can do wonders for your bank account in the future' is pervasive. However, similar to studying solely for the purpose of obtaining a degree, if one studies with the sole intention of securing a future promotion, it undermines the broader rationale of educating oneself for societal, organisational, institutional and personal productivity.

It's crucial to recognise that having a degree, or even an additional degree, does not guarantee the acquisition of a good job, although it could serve as an advantage in the pursuit of employment if the opportunity arises. A degree, in its essence,

 A Job vs Work

is proof that an applicant has undergone formal education and possesses the capacity to learn.

Those who study with the goal of securing a promotion may face challenges in distinguishing between a job and their work. The result of such studies might lead to obtaining a top position within an organisation, riding on the notion of being better trained and more educated than their colleagues. As previously noted, individuals with this mind-set are prone to placing a higher value on their position than the actual work they perform in that role.

Instead of viewing a degree merely as a ticket to higher income, why not adopt a more positive perspective? Consider the achievement not just as a means to additional money but as a tool to acquire knowledge that aids in navigating challenges encountered while on the job. What do you intend to do with all that was taught during your course? Sadly, many students, once they obtain their qualifications, seem to lose interest in applying their knowledge.

More disconcerting are graduates whose academic work was predominantly completed by someone else, possibly even for payment. Such a qualification ends up devoid of value, serving no purpose in making a difference in the graduate's work or the lives of those around them. This phenomenon may explain the presence of supervisors or individuals in high-responsibility positions who lack a genuine understanding of their roles. It suggests that the position was potentially acquired through dubious means, possibly involving corruption.

However, let us not delve into this quagmire and remain focused on the main subject at hand.

Studying for self-pride

Here is the fourth reason why some people choose to pursue education: studying for self-pride. This aligns with various forms of achievement. The knowledge that one has accomplished something, regardless of its scale, can be a significant self-esteem booster for many. However, the impact of this boost largely depends on the nature of the accomplishment and the individual's perception of it.

Some individuals bolster their self-esteem when their goal is to positively influence and enhance the practices of others in their field. Studying can reshape their thinking before they embark on realising their envisioned accomplishments.

In the realm of human behaviour, improvements in self-esteem can yield a substantial impact, both positively and negatively, across various aspects of life. Consider the effects that completing your degree or qualification might bring to you, those around you, and the organisation that employs you. Remember the wisdom of the African Proverb: 'If you fill your head with pride, you will lack space for wisdom.'

Certainly, upon achieving the intended education and fully grasping its content, the likelihood of being overwhelmingly proud of this accomplishment is understandably high. However, just as self-pride can motivate an individual to work harder in their position of employment, it can also lead to the misuse of power, especially towards subordinates. Therefore, understanding the reason behind your educational pursuit is crucial. Establishing a clear motive before taking action plays a significant role in shaping outcomes in life.

An illustrative example emphasises this point. An employee who received a promotion after adding an additional degree to their CV became overconfident, behaving as if he owned the company. The situation escalated to the point where colleagues complained, and the owner had no option but to relieve the individual of his duties. This scenario underscores the potential consequences of an accomplishment, which can either elevate or destroy an individual.

Now, reflect on Chapter Three. Did you enjoy it? Were the questions set at the beginning answered? If you feel that they were not, consider revisiting the chapter. If your answers are positive, get ready to explore Chapter Four. As always, start every chapter by reading and asking yourself the preliminary questions – and own them. Ponder a few of these questions in the summary of Chapter Three that follows.

CHAPTER SUMMARY

- People study for different reasons and each reason can have indirect or direct effects on how one experiences education.
- Of the many reasons that people study, this chapter looked at four of them, namely: to get an education; to earn a degree; to get more money; for self-pride.
- 'Education is an intentional process where a person, as an individual, stands in relation to him- or herself. This happens through two different aspects. The first is his or her individuality and the second is his or her universal essence' (Naziev).
- After achieving an education, you should be able to think independently and thrive in all that you do.
- 'When you create a difference in someone's life, you not only impact their life, you impact everyone influenced by them throughout their entire lifetime. No act is ever too small; one by one, this is how to make an ocean rise' (Danielle Doby).
- 'Education is one of the most powerful things in life. It allows us to find the meaning behind everything and helps improve lives in a massive way' (WB Yeats).
- Barely anyone decides to study with the intention of impacting the lives of people around them, or to be more productive in the job they intend to secure, or in the job they already have.
- There are people whose motive to study is simply to obtain a degree and, as a result, education is unable to transform them.
- Those who study only to earn their degree have no ability to think or see beyond their qualifications.

- Some people study to earn more money and thus have neither made strides nor grown in their organisations.
- Studying only with the intention of getting promoted at some future time defeats the logic behind educating yourself for societal, organisational, institutional and personal productivity.
- When you study for money, you are likely to value your job more than your work and this prevents you from making a difference.
- Studying for self-pride is detrimental in that it may induce a failure to respect colleagues at work or to appreciate their abilities. Instead, it may foster a boastful attitude in the academic about their qualifications and the resulting position they hold.
- Be humble, regardless of how many qualifications you have, and avoid being trapped in the truth of this saying, 'If you fill your head with pride, you will lack space for wisdom' (African Proverb).

4
ADDING VALUE TO YOUR WORK – ITS LEGACY MATTERS

- What is your purpose in life?
- Do you think your work matters?
- How do you add value to your work?
- How does it feel to be praised for the quality of your work?
- Doesn't it feel good when many people praise your work?
- What can you do to improve your work?
- What is the role of your colleague(s) in the work that you do?
- Do you work for a company, for an organisation, for a ministry, for yourself, or for people?

Prioritise adding value to your work! The quality of your output in your current position (your job) is paramount, as it directly influences an organisation or institution's prosperity and operational stability. Moreover, delivering high-quality work contributes to your own sense of independence and stability. Recognising your ability to contribute to a company's growth allows you to cease the constant search for new employment and instead create opportunities for others.

However, the pivotal question remains: Do you know your purpose in life? Have you taken a moment to reflect on what you were born to do, and what you should wholeheartedly pursue while still alive? Many individuals continually search for their life's purpose, a quest often characterised by uncertainty. Oprah Winfrey wisely advises, 'There's no greater gift you can give or receive than to honour your calling. It's why you were born. And how you become most truly alive.'

Helping someone become genuinely productive is challenging if they are not in harmony with their true purpose. In today's world, individuals who pursue education for employment may find that discovering their true purpose becomes an elusive dream. We have long abandoned effective career guidance programs that once helped students determine the best course of study at universities or other tertiary education institutions. Initially, students might have been driven by the ambition to develop a God-given gift or pursued courses aligned with their personal beliefs or interests.

Today, the primary motivation for most – perhaps all – students to graduate is to acquire a certificate, diploma or degree with the sole purpose of securing employment. However, as explored in Chapter Three, prioritising a job as the main motivation for enrolling in a course can have detrimental effects in the long run.

Consider this: The government may not be capable of absorbing all graduate teachers or nurses, and those absorbed into state-owned enterprises are encouraged to transition to new roles after a certain period, creating opportunities for others. This approach can alleviate unemployment and broaden the country's employment avenues.

However, the reality is that many individuals prioritise the need for employment. The current system is saturated, with employees, especially those in government positions for over ten years, being reluctant to leave. When asked about leaving their jobs, they often express a lack of consideration for such a possibility. They may respond by asking where they would go and what they would do if they left.

It was on a Friday morning during our end-of-the-week staff briefing when a senior colleague was given a chance to pray before the briefing started. She began, and somewhere in her prayer she said: 'Lord, You are nothing without me.' I tell you, the whole staff laughed and almost everyone had something to say about it for the rest of that day.

Certainly, she must have intended to say: 'Lord, I am nothing without you.' After the briefing, I approached her and reminded her of the prayer that had elicited laughter from the entire staff. I said, 'Ma'am, don't you think it's time for you to go and rest? The fact that you taught some of the young teachers here is proof that you have played a significant role in this profession. Taking a break and enjoying your pension would be beneficial. The slip-up today during the prayer suggests you might be tired and in need of rest.'

And what was her response? She said, 'Mr. Sebastian [pseudonym], I am not tired; I am still strong and capable of teaching. Can you recall a day when you saw me falter at work? What would I do at home?'

This prompted another round of laughter between the two of us.

This situation vividly illustrates why many people cling to their jobs, regardless of their productivity and effectiveness. Unfortunately, even recently graduated teachers hope for government employment, while senior teachers persist in their roles until a notable work failure signals that it's time to retire. This phenomenon is not exclusive to the public sector; it's prevalent in the private sector as well. Consider the question: How long will you wait?

Much unhappiness stems from a failure to discover one's life purpose. As Munroe (2007:32) stated, 'The greatest tragedy is not death but living life without purpose'. This underscores the importance of first discovering your purpose and secondly continually improving your work within or towards that purpose.

Some individuals remain in their jobs until retirement or even until death separates them from their roles. Could there have been ways to improve what they were doing during that extended period? This question is crucial for those still seeking employment. There are numerous ways to add value to one's work that would benefit the employer. One approach is to ensure that whatever you produce holds significance. With each task, ask yourself: How can I add value that benefits others, my employer, and myself? This mind-set fosters diligence and a commitment to striving for perfection.

Another approach is to maintain an unwavering level of integrity. Sakaria Nikodemus aptly defines integrity as 'doing the right thing even when nobody is watching you'. The absence of integrity among those in leadership roles has led to broken homes, sour relationships, failed businesses, collapsed organisations and struggling economies in many countries. Employees must safeguard their integrity to uphold or elevate the desired standards of their work production.

Integrity has always been the key to an individual's good reputation, and it significantly influences a company's growth and the services it provides.

Augustinus M. Ngombe adds his perspective on how integrity becomes relevant for our benefit. He says:

> Integrity is a leadership trait which ensures that a leader remains true to themselves and that there is always merit in what they say and do. It is this practice that encourages followers to believe in their leader's trustworthiness. Leaders with high integrity do not go about making promises before

they have done proper assessments and are assured of being able to deliver. They are rare gems in the political strata, but are common among community leaders. Our country and communities have, increasingly, been duped by multiple leaders who lack integrity, hence the struggles we are now facing.

Leaders who have integrity are ethical too. It is almost impossible to possess integrity without principles or ethics. A good example of such a man is, of course, Nelson Mandela. Countless times, he was offered money and high positions, and even an early release from prison, if he relinquished his push for freedom and denounced the fight against apartheid. He was consistent in his response, which was that 'Deals are only negotiated by free men. I cannot be free if everyone else is not free.' In other words, he walked his talk and talked his walk.

In contrast, those without integrity prosper at the expense of others. Such are most of our local political leaders who are quick to make empty promises during their campaigns but, immediately they are in their new offices, they forget about the people who put them in power. These unethical leaders who lack integrity may also be our employers, the ones who also change their talk depending on whom they are dealing with at a given time.

Under this kind of leadership, people are undermined, poverty increases and organisations or communities remain undeveloped.

Certainly, when you genuinely value your work and appreciate what you do – along with respecting the position you currently hold or may find yourself in – there are certain actions you should avoid if you aim to preserve your personal integrity and principles. Noble character traits set individuals apart and, although not everyone possesses them, those who do stand out above the crowd. It's crucial to keep striving for good character traits and honour them, regardless of the circumstances.

For further exploration on this subject, the Global Career Hub (see references) identifies five additional ways employees can add value to their work and contribute to their employers.

Be a keen problem solver

Employees who are eager to find creative solutions to business problems add value to their employers. Being able to find a solution to a problem can give businesses a competitive edge, especially if it allows employees to focus on other issues. An example of this might be finding a solution to meet a project deadline earlier than expected, allowing you and your team to turn your attention elsewhere.

Consider the experience of an individual described above. We, as humans, are drawn to role players who demonstrate that problems can often be resolved by ordinary people – individuals not vastly different from those who created the issues in the first place. By embodying the role of a problem solver within a company, not only do you benefit the owner(s) of the company, but you also contribute positively to your colleagues and the clients served by the company.

Within a business or company, such a problem-solving individual is perceived as a real asset, not a liability. The presence of a problem solver in the company eliminates the need to hire external professionals for tasks that one of their own employees can adeptly handle. This dynamic is especially beneficial for the company.

Conversely, for businesses that lack proactive problem solvers within their ranks, the situation may be different. The need to hire external professionals might be more prevalent in such cases.

Show initiative

Being able to pick up tasks – as required or even without being asked – is a trait that many employers value. Showing initiative and helping team members during busy periods of business will not only benefit your employer but will put you in good standing with your team. If you are aware that one of your colleagues is struggling to get through their workload, offering to help will be well perceived by your colleagues and show your employer that you do not have only your own interests in mind.

The chances of having people – who are worth emulating – with such characteristics in any workplace could be quite high. The problem arises when they ask what they will get in return before they go that extra mile, before they go beyond what is mandated for their given responsibilities.

Our human nature dictates that we work continuously, that we keep busy, even when the specifics or quantity of what we will do is not yet clear. This suggests that people will be productive without expecting anything in return; that they will love producing even simply by using their hands, or simply through the application of their knowledge and skills.

If the spirit of expectation before doing anything is resisted, a lot of potential and initiative could be unleashed and put to practical use. So much is hampered by this selfishness, which tends to have very detrimental effects.

Continually look for improvements

Time is money. If you can develop ways of improving productivity and increasing your efficiency, you add value by saving your employer's valuable resources. This could come from streamlining a process within the business, or by finding solutions for partnering with internal teams on budgeting and forecasting.

Consider a business that extracts more value from the resources it already possesses. This approach is akin to applying the logic of getting the most out of what is available in the business arsenal. Often, businesses experience significant losses because creative minds are not actively engaged and fail to explore innovative ways to enhance various operations.

For instance, if a company faces substantial time losses because supervisors need to address their subordinates in person, a simple yet effective solution could be providing every employee with a smartphone to access company emails and messages. Numerous examples resonate with this point, highlighting missed opportunities for improvement.

It's crucial to note that implementing such improvements not only benefits the business by saving time and money but also enhances the individual employee experience. For instance, giving employees tools to access organisational schedules can significantly aid those struggling to stay abreast of company timelines.

However, it's essential for employees to reciprocate by consistently improving their productivity to ensure that the business doesn't incur deficits due to these initiatives. This collaborative effort fosters a win-win situation where both the business and its employees thrive.

Keep your technical skills up to date

When they are looking to hire for a new position, employers seek professionals with current skills, but they also prefer candidates who keep up to date with relevant regulation and industry changes while they are in the role. Stay abreast of new regulations while in your job by attending courses and webinars to keep your skills current. Search for institutions that offer training and courses that can help further your qualifications and develop your technical skill set. This is certain to improve the quality of the work you do.

Learning is an endless journey, a constant process that accompanies us every day throughout our lives. It persists until our final breath, as we exist in a dynamic world that continually presents new challenges, demanding innovative thinking and the application of knowledge acquired over time. The concept of Continuing Professional Development (CPD) encapsulates our ongoing efforts to stay informed and equipped with the skills required to navigate the complexities of today's world, enabling us to function with competence.

Some scholars aptly describe the current state of our world as a VUCA World. VUCA stands for volatility, uncertainty, complexity, and ambiguity – a fitting acronym when viewed in the context of our ongoing discussion. These terms encapsulate the constant and unpredictable changes that have become the norm in specific industries and sectors of the business world. Effectively responding to these challenges requires a continuous commitment to expanding our knowledge and skills, ensuring that we remain equipped to navigate the ever-evolving landscape.

Improve your communication skills

For instance, the role of accounting and finance has evolved and now plays a wider role in business. Employers expect finance professionals to communicate confidently with other departments in the business. Improving communication skills allows professionals to interact more effectively within the business when they present results or suggest innovative solutions.

Professionals who are able to communicate findings and explain their impact in a way that others in the business will understand are valuable to employers and to their work. Strategies for improving communication skills include public speaking courses, volunteering to draft memos, or leading meetings.

Successful professionals are always on the lookout for ways to advance their careers and enhance their skill sets continually. Regularly assessing whether you are meeting your employer's expectations and finding ways to improve your productivity is a beneficial practice. Why? When it comes to remuneration and career advancement, demonstrating that you have gone above and beyond expectations is the most effective way to achieve both.

Articulating how your work has added value to a company, backed by examples, becomes crucial when negotiating a pay rise or career development. Remember, jobs may come and go, but the impact of your work will endure, either physically or through the acclaim of those who benefit from it. Be intentional in all that you do in your job or at work.

For context, consider your profession. If you are a teacher or aspiring to be one, how do you plan to add value to your teaching profession and the Ministry of Education? If you are a nurse or aspiring to become one, what are your plans to leave a lasting positive impression on the nursing profession? Apply this reflective approach to any other profession or job. Consider how you can add value and benefit your employer.

Two important principles to remember are never to procrastinate when given a task and never to compare yourself negatively to a colleague. Instead, be a positive force, provide intentional advice, and possibly change your colleague's mindset to view their role more positively.

Employees should focus on looking up to hardworking colleagues and striving to emulate them. Adding value to your work is crucial because, just as your employer matters to you, you matter to your employer, and your work matters even more. Keep this two-way relationship mutually beneficial.

I trust you've taken note of the strategies to add value to your work and benefit your employer. You can take pride in reaching the end of this chapter. As you embark on Chapter Five, mentally preparing yourself and reviewing the preliminary questions before continuing is a recommended practice.

CHAPTER SUMMARY

- Prioritise the quality of the work you produce, as it significantly influences the success and stability of an organisation or institution, serving as a vital aspect of your role in the position you hold (your job).
- Recognise your capabilities in contributing to the growth of a company or organisation. Knowing your potential allows you to confidently cease job hunting and start creating employment opportunities for others.
- The quality of your work provides a sense of independence and stability in your professional journey.
- 'There's no greater gift you can give or receive than to honour your calling. It's why you were born. And how you become most truly alive' (Oprah Winfrey).
- It becomes challenging to assist others in becoming productively aligned if they are out of harmony with their life's purpose.
- A job should not be the top reason for enrolling in a course, as this motive can have detrimental effects in the long run.
- Knowing when to resign and open up employment opportunities for others is crucial when you are employed.
- Recognise the signs when your energy and productivity diminish due to a loss of interest. Leaving your job at this point can be essential to prevent personal degeneration and organisational risks.
- Human beings possess problem-solving capabilities. Be an asset to your employers, colleagues and those you serve.
- Love and value your work to the extent that your company or organisation would find it challenging, if not virtually impossible, to replace you. Strive to be irreplaceable.

- Avoid procrastination, as it has the potential to diminish the standing of prominent individuals and large organisations.
- Never cease learning, as life gains significance with increased awareness of surroundings and challenges. Continuous learning equips us to navigate difficulties and find solutions.
- Communicate openly and share relevant information because knowledge is power, benefitting both you and others.

5
MISPLACEMENT AT WORK

- Do you think some people are misplaced in their workplace?
- Does your work make you feel misplaced?
- Who do you think misplaced you: your employer or yourself?
- How do you make sure not to be misplaced?
- Are you satisfied with what you do at your workplace?

Have you set your expectations for this chapter? Good. Let's begin with this rhetorical question: Have you ever noticed someone underperforming at work or in their job, and could it possibly be you?

Note that there is always someone doing something contrary to their likes, desires or personal wants. Nikodemus (2010:71) states that some people underperform not because they are incompetent, but simply because they find themselves doing what they are, in fact, not good at.

Further questions arising around this subject include: Do you have a misplaced employee? Are you, as an employee, misplaced? This brings us to the topic of the misplacement of individuals in their workplaces.

Remember that Chapter Three investigated certain reasons why people study nowadays, and you should not be surprised that some people are misplaced at their workplaces. Who are these people? Imagine that you studied engineering, and you ended up doing clerical work. Imagine that you were trained as a nurse, and you ended up doing something completely different.

Another aspect of this is that some people may decide to undergo, or have undergone, training or studied courses that are far removed from their aspirations or abilities. It means that you will encounter certain people who have committed themselves through tertiary education or training to become 'this' or 'that', but their choices may have been made because the course could easily and quickly secure them a job after completion. Do you know that the education or teaching profession attracts ambitious people who are not true teachers? This is especially noticeable in developing countries and perhaps even more so in underdeveloped countries. Do you still wonder why? You should not!

Although misplacement may be in the field of study or at work, some people still manage to be good and productive within their misplaced areas of work, or may still get good grades in their misplaced fields of study. This is made possible by being humble, committed, dedicated and through an endeavour for personal development. It is helped by studying hard and smart – even those who did courses for misinformed reasons – and working hard and having a wholehearted approach to their work – even those who are misplaced at workplaces. Such employees may even get promoted in their misplaced jobs.

Interestingly, some people get themselves misplaced by applying for a job – and getting it – that does not really match their competencies, but their qualifications match the job requirements. However, because of their lack of commitment, dedication and love for what they do, they end up losing that job.

It should be vividly clear that such people live among us; you might even be one of them. The best course of action is, therefore, to help make their situations easier instead of condemning them for being misplaced or for misplacing themselves. If employers want increased productivity in their organisation or company, they should understand that certain jobs are what potentially motivate students to take certain courses and seek certain employment – it is not their desire to make a difference to society. Such employers need to know that something must be done.

And what can they do, then? It is very simple: they should observe their employees and notice what they do well at. Should they see someone struggling, arrange to have a private chat at an appropriate time and place – perhaps during a staff meeting – if they do not mind. Ask them whether they, in their individual capacity, are happy doing what they are doing and, if not, allow them to suggest what could lift their morale and allow them to work wholeheartedly. Interactions like this would increase the employee's productivity, benefitting both themselves and the company or organisation.

Another idea that could be initiated is to have a suggestion box where employees – and clients or customers – could identify problems within the organisation or company or its employees and suggest improvements. Employees' attitudes are often described best by customers or clients. It is also important for management to realise how worthwhile in-service training and workshops are to both the employees, the supervisors and to employers themselves. Remember that a happy employee is a productive employee, and the benefit is mostly for employers and for those who make use of the services of their employees.

For employees, remember that you were not employed primarily for a salary but to make a difference to those who benefit from your work. Therefore, you should find joy in offering your best service to whomever approaches you at work. Should you feel that you cannot do your best in your current position, but believe you could do better in a different position with similar responsibilities, do open up and explain this to your employer or immediate superior.

Your employer or supervisors are, if nothing else, there to help you serve their clients or customers, whom you were, after all, employed to serve. Do explain your dilemma to your superior in the most appropriate place and as soon as possible.

It becomes unrealistic for your employer to hold onto you if you occupy a position in their organisation or company without being productive, efficient and effective. It simply means that you are stealing time, resources and money from your employer while depriving the public of accessing products or services in the correct and appropriate way.

When the relationship between employer and employee is good, the result is mutually beneficial, and the business or company thrives in terms of both productivity and profitability. It is important for employees to be shown that their employer or supervisor cares and is always willing to listen to them. They should not be nervous or reserved when they approach their supervisors or employers but should rather view them as partners in a mutual effort to help the organisation survive and grow.

In truth, the company or business cannot function unless their employees are dedicated to their work, and the employees cannot afford to be without the employment they have secured. However, working well together can only be achieved by acceptance and respect, and knowing that each party is worth keeping for the benefit of the other. Embrace the notion of 'I am because you are' because it is critically important in every given organisation or business. Find unity of purpose in the people you work with, balance every strength with every weakness and every weakness with every strength.

An employee who is misplaced can be devastating to an organisation and quite draining for the misplaced individual. As an employee, always try to assess and reassess your activities at work, establishing how beneficial they are both to yourself and to the organisation. It is not helpful to pay undue attention to the type of job you have. Rather pay attention to how best to perform your duties while in that job.

While employees should correct their attitude towards their work and to the companies or organisations that gave them their jobs, employers should, equally, boost their relationships with their employees by demonstrating a caring attitude, even love. Happiness in the workplace yields productivity in a business and growth in individuals. This could extend outside the workplace and touch on different aspects of lives, since more time is often spent at work than at leisure.

That was Chapter Five. How did you find it? Has it introduced you to what could help in changing your attitude towards your work and help you never to believe that misplacement at your job or place of employment is an insoluble problem? I hope you now know what to do should you find yourself in that frame of mind.

You are about to feel like an achiever, a conqueror, for you are left with only two chapters. Chapter Six is the second-last in this book. As always, take time to go through the preliminary questions because they give you a general impression of what the chapter has in store for you. Good luck!

CHAPTER SUMMARY

- Every employee should be able to do their best within the ambit of their duties. The same is true for employers. Once you have made the decision to be an employer, do whatever is best for your business, the company, and for all those for whom you created employment.

- Some people underperform, not because they are incompetent but simply because they find themselves doing what they are not actually good at.

- The education or teaching profession is one of those that rescues many individuals who struggle to find deserving jobs, as per their qualifications. Hence, the profession may host a high number of misplacements.

- Misplaced or not misplaced? A difference is made by humbleness, commitment, dedication and personal development.

- The fact is that many people study for reasons other than to achieve their true calling. Misplacements have become common in almost every sphere of life. Note that one may have the correct qualifications as specified on an advertisement for a particular job, but may not be competent enough to execute the duties as required.

- In-service training may be a problem solver in changing the narratives that come with job or work misplacements. Ensure that you, as an employee, keep abreast of what underpins the work you do for your employers. And you, as an employer, make sure your employees are given the right support because it could enable them to perform wonders in your company or organisation.

- For employees, you were employed to serve and not for your salary. Note that what you earn comes as a result of what you do, so do it better!
- Employers, please check up on your employees, aim for a better workplace spirit and foster a mutual connection. This is vital for the growth of your business.
- Let the suggestions given by employees lead the way for you; let them direct the steps you take.
- Develop a mind-set that respects the existence of a business or company and the existence of all who strive to make it thrive.
- Employers must see their employees as partners in business for in their unity lies the power for the business to thrive.

6
TRADING ON PERSONA AND NOT ON QUALIFICATIONS

- What is an academic qualification?
- Do you know that the qualification you have can also be obtained by other people?
- Why do you think one person gets a job when another person who has the same qualification does not get that job?
- Have you ever come across someone who does things the same way as another person?
- Do you know that you are unique, that there is no one else like you?
- How do personal character traits affect your job performance or your work?
- How are positive character traits admired?
- How do negative personal character traits hinder your career?
- Do you know that your personality is the game changer?

While many people focus on building their personal profiles by improving their character traits, others stagnate and become irrelevant in competitive job markets. The purpose of this chapter is to remind us that numerous people have similar degrees to ours, some with even better grades, and an academic qualification should be treated as a document that simply proves you can be schooled, and not as a ticket to securing a job. A different and more reliable way of job seeking is to put your qualification aside and market your unique values and principles. Whereas listing your qualifications may not be enough in today's competitive world, you could be the only applicant with certain attributes that are requirements for a particular job.

Guide, build and protect your unique character traits because it is through them that you stand out above other people. You may have heard about – or even met – someone who has achieved only a high school certificate, or not even that, but who works alongside colleagues with several higher or advanced academic degrees, or with certificates from tertiary education institutions. It is sure to be the character traits of the less qualified person that make them a valuable asset to their employer and put them on an equal footing with those colleagues.

Kurtus (2021) writes about the importance of your character in building a career:

> Your character consists of attitudes you have toward challenges you face in your career. Good character is important in your career. Having positive character traits will improve your chances of success and in achieving your goals. Negative traits hinder your efforts and your job performance.

Performance factors. Personal character traits are sometimes called your work ethic. They concern your attitudes towards, for instance, performing difficult tasks, fulfilling requirements and specifications, following orders, being organised and working up to your capabilities. There are other factors that make up your personal character traits and indirectly affect your ability to complete tasks and achieve goals; they include the manner in which you spend your money or take care of your body. These can also influence your performance.

Positive traits admired. Having positive character traits means that you are able and willing to do good work, both for your own satisfaction and for your employer's. These traits relate to your attitude towards challenges at work. Typical traits are: determination, ability to organise, courage and responsibility.

Moreover, the ability to communicate effectively, work in a team and adapt to changes are also highly valued traits in the workplace. Employers often seek individuals who not only possess the necessary technical skills but also exhibit strong interpersonal and adaptability skills. These qualities contribute to a positive work environment and enhance overall team dynamics.

> Harry had an assignment that needed to be completed by Friday. It was a difficult task, but he was not afraid to work hard to complete it. His boss knew Harry would commit to it because he had the type of character that compelled him to overcome difficulties and achieve goals. When Harry had completed the assignment, the boss gave him recognition for a job well done.

Good performances is the result of a good work ethic and employers seek workers who have positive personal character traits.

Negative traits not wanted. Negative personal character traits include carelessness, sloth, and irresponsibility.

> Phillip was a highly skilled worker, but he was often careless in what he did. He figured his work was good enough, especially when he wasn't too interested in the task. Sometimes his work had to be done over by someone else. Although Phillip

was talented and skilled, he was a drag on his department's proposed bottom line and was ultimately discharged.

These negative character traits or attitudes can hinder your ability to achieve goals or to satisfy job requirements. Employers typically do not advance workers with negative character traits.

If your personal character includes the attitudes you have toward challenges in your career, having positive traits will improve your performance and chances of success while negative traits will hinder your efforts. Understand the impact of character traits on your work and ultimately on your career.

Hopefully, the explanations given by Kurtus helped to dispel any misconceptions you may have had and have shown you how character traits can supersede the possession of qualifications.

People who secure a job sometimes belittle the struggle they had to get it. This can affect their job performance if, for instance, after landing the job they resort to relaxing at work. This relates to Kurtus's warning not to submit to your negative traits because, instead of improving your performance and chances of success, you hinder those chances. An employer is unlikely to promote lax employees or may choose to keep them in the position in which they started out – and never raise their pay either.

Since the dream of every employee is to climb the ladder of success in their given career, it is vital to maintain good discipline, focus and commitment at work. As a guide, here are some tips – extracted from the website Glassdoor – which may be helpful.

Ten Important Character Traits that Enhance Work Performance

1. **Communication Skills:** Effective communication is crucial in any workplace. Employees who can articulate their thoughts clearly, listen actively and convey information in a concise manner are very valuable. Good communicators can avoid misunderstandings, foster collaboration and contribute to a positive work environment.
2. **Team Player:** Being a team player is essential for success in most workplaces. Employees who can collaborate, share ideas and work effectively with others contribute to a harmonious work environment. Employers appreciate individuals who prioritise the success of the team over personal achievements.
3. **Time Management:** Efficient time management is a key trait for productivity. Employees who can prioritise tasks, set deadlines and complete assignments in a timely manner contribute to the overall success of the organisation. Effective time management helps in meeting goals and preventing delays.
4. **Problem-Solving Skills:** The ability to analyse situations, identify challenges and propose effective solutions is very valuable. Employees who can think critically and offer innovative solutions contribute to the growth and success of the company. Problem-solving skills are crucial for overcoming obstacles and achieving objectives.
5. **Adaptability:** In a dynamic work environment, adaptability is a valuable trait. Employees who can embrace change, learn new skills and adjust to evolving situations are assets to the organisation. Adaptability is essential in industries where technology and market conditions are rapidly changing.

6. **Leadership Qualities:** Even if not in a formal leadership role, having leadership qualities such as initiative, decisiveness and the ability to motivate others is advantageous. Employees who can lead by example, inspire their colleagues and take charge when needed contribute to a positive and effective workplace.

7. **Negotiation Skills:** Negotiation skills are valuable in various professional scenarios, such as contract discussions, resolving conflicts or reaching agreements. Employees who can negotiate effectively, finding common ground and securing favourable outcomes, are assets to their teams and organisations.

8. **Networking Abilities:** Building professional relationships inside and outside the company is crucial for career development. Individuals with strong networking abilities can connect with colleagues, clients and industry professionals, opening up opportunities for collaboration, mentorship and career advancement.

9. **Tech Savviness:** In the modern workplace, being comfortable with technology is increasingly important. Employees who can adapt to new software, tools and digital platforms contribute to increased efficiency and can facilitate the integration of technology into various aspects of the business.

10. **Resilience:** Resilience involves bouncing back from setbacks and maintaining a positive attitude in the face of challenges. Employees who can navigate stress, setbacks, or failures with resilience demonstrate emotional intelligence and contribute to a healthy workplace culture.

It is unlikely that the tips given here can be learned within the confines of a classroom's four walls. Hence, this is a tangible reason why trading on your noble and unique personal traits is more important than relying on documents – pieces of paper – showing results that others may surpass. If you have always believed that qualifications are the game changer – that having a degree is the ultimate determining factor for future career advancement – I suggest you change your mind-set and become more reliant on personal qualities, striving to improve yours as soon and as much as possible.

When you work on your personal qualities, you can be absolutely sure that no one else possesses the same qualities as you do. We say: 'There is no one like Jesus,' and surely, there is no one like you. You are unique, and your uniqueness is the best tool you can use to find a job. Perhaps you have once, or even several times, heard people say that the first thing they noticed about someone was their attitude towards other people. Again, this convinces us not to underrate the need to develop whatever it is that defines our uniqueness.

Although it may come across as censorious, I must mention that many people have been dismissed because of their bad attitude, not only towards their work but also to their colleagues, supervisors, and/or employers. Qualifications bear no relationship to people's attitudes and actions. What matters is how much damage difficult employees can do to an organisation and how their inability to work with others might negatively influence their ability to become significant in the organisation, as well as in their colleagues' lives.

Employees may think that their qualifications guarantee their job security, but the reality is that qualifications might also promote unnecessary infighting. Questions may be asked, like: Why is this person here if he failed high school? How can they be promoted when they have just started working? NO! This is corruption! Such unsettling situations at work have led to employees receiving unnecessary warnings. Some situations can get so awful that employees lose their jobs, or they get into physical fights and then also lose their jobs.

I would never condone or promote corrupt acts at the workplace but rather encourage you to focus on doing what is right at work. This behaviour could help you climb ladders within your career. Many employees spend time doing what does not benefit them or anyone else; instead, they should do whatever is best with the resources at their disposal.

Strive also to change your attitude to people with different backgrounds and understand that they often bring unusual skills to the workplace, which can be learned and mastered by every other individual. At work, there are no mysterious methods used by others that are not available to you.

Instead of asking questions that are belittling and negative about close colleagues who are getting ahead, examine their commitment levels, their sense of responsibility, the way they approach tasks given to them, how well they fit into a team, what motivates them at work, how much they value their work, whether they tend to change every negative thing about their job into something positive, how they do not brandish their qualifications to influence what happens at work. Examine what they do, and how and why they do it. You could discover reasons why your employers treat you and them differently.

Put your pride aside and cultivate a positive attitude towards everyone and everything at work. Holding grudges against your colleagues, supervisors or your employer is not conducive to a healthy atmosphere. Talk openly about your problems and address them before they escalate, causing more issues for you, your colleagues and the company that employs you.

The ability to determine how the day could be structured to benefit you and your co-workers may be just what you lack to get to the top. Try a different approach, but let it be different in good faith. Your colleagues need the positive you, and your employer needs your forward-looking personality because, for the organisation or company to grow, it needs healthy relationships in the workplace. The same applies to the relationships between employees and customers.

To reiterate, trade on your personal qualities and not just your qualifications. You were not born with that paper, nor were you raised with it. If the qualification you have is also possessed by another person, think of different ways to stand out from others, knowing that this is achievable only by honing your personal traits. Work, therefore, on what makes you unique, and then you too shall rise and excel.

CHAPTER SUMMARY

- In today's world, an academic qualification is no longer a guarantee to securing a job. This, however, does not mean that you should not study. NO! It simply means that you should go beyond what can be obtained from a course. Think outside the content of your course and continue developing yourself, but remain humble.

- Have a peaceful kind of nature, and guard and protect it, for this establishes your uniqueness among many peers or other groups of people.

- You must surely have come across a successful person without high school or tertiary qualifications; someone who displays incredible morals and a character worth emulating. This shows how important character is over a qualification.

- 'Your character consists of the attitudes you have toward the challenges you face in your career. Good character is important in your career. Having positive character traits will improve your chances of success and of achieving your goals. Negative traits hinder your efforts and your job performance' (Kurtus 2021).

- Positive traits must be admired, just as negative traits must be abhorred. Try to conquer those if you do have them.

- Because the dream of employees is to see themselves climb the ladder of success in their given career, it is pertinent for them to maintain good discipline and commitment at work.

- Do not forget to develop characteristics that enhance work performance for both your own personal and your organisation's growth.

- What defines us cannot usually be found within a classroom's four walls, but we can learn from one another and, yes, we can develop our characters by becoming intentional in how we would like to be identified.

- Your attitude is what a person you meet first sees in you, and you can choose whether to display a positive or a negative attitude towards others. We mirror one another, thus through another's observation we can glimpse our true essence.

- People may have similar qualifications; the difference between them is their attitude and the character they display when facing challenges. Understand this, for it helps you accept that such differences may be what gets others ahead of you.

- Do not ask belittling and negative questions about work colleagues who are making progress. Rather look at their level of commitment, their sense of responsibility, the way they approach tasks given to them, how well they fit into a team, what motivates them at work, how much they value their work, how they tend to change every negative thing about their job into something positive and how they do not brandish their qualifications. Success is all about what, how and why.

- All along, your inability to determine how best the day could be spent for both you and your co-workers may be just what has stopped you from getting to the top. Try a different approach, and be different in good faith, for your colleagues need the positive you and your employer needs your forward-looking personality.

- It is not worth putting a healthy work environment at risk by holding grudges against your colleagues, your supervisors or your employer.

7

THE SURVIVAL OF BUSINESSES/ORGANISATIONS DEPENDS ON ITS EMPLOYERS AND EMPLOYEES

- Should customers be blamed for business failures?
- What should employers do to stay afloat?
- What is the role of employees in the success of a business?
- Can a business exist without an employer, employees and customers?

The questions in this chapter aim to give you some idea of what and how a business or an organisation should operate while valuing all its role players. It is, indeed, vital to understand that for a business to function, certain things need to be viewed holistically. The content of this chapter is based on and directed by these questions.

Blame not the customers

When things are not going well, businesses frequently point fingers at their customers. This narrative needs to change because customers just play along in tune with the way the business operates. In other words, if a business values its customers and regards them as a priority, the customers will be loyal and probably recommend the business to friends and acquaintances. When things go in the opposite direction, the converse is true.

A common mistake is to think that customers have simply decided not to buy from your business and leave the thinking there. Instead, both business owners and communities who use the services or the products offered by this particular business would benefit if the owners, after noticing the business's decline, sat around a table to figure out the problem. They could strategise, contemplate alternatives and solve the problem by applying the best of the available solutions.

The same applies to educational institutions or schools, in which the learners or students are the customers. What happens in most schools when grades drop is that teachers and managers blame the learners or, at times, their parents. They do not approach the issue as a whole; they do not acknowledge what went wrong and identify its cause. They need to discover what factors were responsible for the problem and decide how to tackle them to improve future outcomes. When managers and staff point fingers and ignore their own culpability, a fortune in resources is potentially lost.

If we do not admit and rectify problems soon enough, resources will continue to be lost both in businesses and in schools or other educational institutions.

It is simple. A business's customer base declines for four reasons: the way employers treat employees; the way employees treat customers; from an increase in competition; from a decrease in the quality of the product offered or the services rendered. One or two of these may affect what a business experiences. Schools deteriorate because results depend on the input of the school (teachers, heads of departments and principals), on the learners themselves, and on the parents. Any of these affect the performances of the learners and ultimately the success of the school.

Do not expect improved results when the wrong done by the teachers, heads of departments, principals, learners and parents is not corrected. We must acknowledge and do something about the problems because acting as if they do not exist or we do not know how to handle them will not yield positive results.

Employers empowering employees

Who are the employers or business owners? The obvious response is, 'Those who establish and own businesses'. Yes, they are, but the crystal-clear truth is that supervisors and managers are often seen and treated as employers. Why do I say so? Let me explain!

Have you noticed how supervisors are labelled, how their subordinates often falsely accuse them of conspiring with the owners of businesses? For those employees, a supervisor represents the owner of the business when the actual owner is absent. There is some degree of truth in their perception because supervisors must do whatever they can for the sake of the business or organisation. However, it is not necessary nor ethical for them to treat their subordinates harshly.

Every supervisor or manager is empowered by their employer and entrusted with responsibilities that should optimise the functioning of the business or organisation. This empowerment gives them the status of substitute business owners in the eyes of their subordinates. Importantly, the rest of the staff should also feel empowered. Why should this be the case? It is because employees are in direct contact with the customers and if they feel empowered, they will treat customers with the requisite respect and care.

Try making this observation. One day enter a business premises and observe how employees interact with customers. What you see will definitely reflect the kind of treatment they receive from their supervisors, managers or the owners of the business or organisation. You don't need to convince people to buy from you; rather, treat your employees with respect and the dignity they deserve, and then they shall do the rest for you.

This is also an interesting thing to do: Go to a school and ask – or observe – which of the teachers spend most of the time yelling, shouting, beating and calling learners rude names. Find out how those teachers view the school's management, its administration, the parents and/or learners, and the teachers themselves. There is a 99% likelihood that these teachers lack any interest in improving either the school or the learners' performances. They probably blame everyone else for whatever is going wrong at the school.

It is imperative that both schools and businesses treat employees and teachers well and that any problems are aired and then addressed in an amicable way. This will reduce the potential for both employees and teachers to vent their frustration on the customers of ordinary businesses and on learners at schools. Customers should not be privy to an employee's frustrations as that would negatively affect their relationship with the business. Likewise, learners must not see or feel their teachers' frustration as this affects their performance and encourages absenteeism. It also increases their chances of dropping out of school.

If anything, a school should be a place of refuge for every learner and a place of caring for every teacher. Every threatened and fearful learner does not learn, and every frustrated teacher does not care and, in the end, we will lose the meaning and understanding behind the concept of schooling.

Employees own the business or run the institution

What has been said above gives us an irrefutable reason why employees should be treated with respect. Spoil them if need be because these people are at the heart of the business or organisation. By this, I mean that it is they who are actually in control – although generally we believe it to be the supervisors.

If you have doubts about this, imagine yourself as a manager, supervisor or owner of the business, standing in front of your employees. What would happen if you asked the employees or teachers to do something and they did not buy into your request? How would this make you feel? Would you feel you had better stop talking? Yes, you would feel that, not because you are incompetent but simply because it is those guys who are in charge, and your role is only to provide guidance and support. Retaliating, being unyielding, and not recognising the nobility of the role employees play in all the operations of a business or organisation will worsen the situation. The more you, as a leader in their midst, push for what you want them to do, the more you will be ignored. Later, you will feel as if your authority has been undermined, and your anger might make you hurt them even more.

The above reinforces the well-known statement about leaders who don't listen being surrounded by people who have nothing to say. I have seen this, and I have experienced it, and continue to do so. I am sure you have too. If not yet, you will surely see it or be told about it one day.

If you are a leader, I hope you study and understand the environment in which you operate, and that you know when people have had enough of your methods. I hope that you will be able to adjust and begin to sympathise and reason with them. Understanding signs from people is neither complex nor rocket science; one is able to see and feel the signs. Unfortunately, many leaders or managers choose to ignore clear signals and continue to push inconsiderately for what they believe needs to be done.

Let us build an environment based on the premise that people do not care what you know or do or have but are more concerned about how you make them feel. This is a very powerful statement and one, if embraced by both employees and employers or supervisors, should ensure that the working relationships of these groups are unlikely to be compromised. All that matters is how to get them involved, how to support them, and how to guide them. The rest usually falls into place.

Employers, employees and customers are all key players

Everyone involved in, or who is part of, a business or organisation is as important as all the others, regardless of their capacity. Have you observed that those who feel fairly treated at their place of work are not concerned with the differences between them and their colleagues in terms of their roles? They understand their own positions and that of others. Treatment that is universally bad will always be bad, just as good will always be good.

The simple sequence is:

- Employers acknowledge that they are called employers because people are ready to be employed and be called employees.
- Employees know that they are called employees because they are employed to serve the customers to the best of their abilities.

The bottom line is that respect, love and care should reign for everyone; it should flow from the bottom to the top and from the top to the bottom.

CHAPTER SUMMARY

- Blame not the customers or clients for the failures of your business, organisation or institution as they simply respond to the tunes played by the operators of the business or organisation.

- As a business owner, you should introspect to best understand the origin of the problem that the business may be facing.

- Treat every customer and client as noble, for they have the power either to tarnish or to promote your business.

- In business, a decline in customers can only result from: how employers treat employees; how employees treat customers; an increase in competition; or a decrease in the quality of the product or services rendered.

- In educational institutions, learners, teachers, principals, heads of departments, parents, the community and the relevant ministry are equally responsible for the functioning of their schools and for the performances of their learners.

- The supervisor, manager or person in authority may not necessarily be the business owner. Relative to employees, they simply play representative and supervisory roles in order to make things operate efficiently within the business or organisation.

- The way business owners, supervisors or managers treat ordinary employees is reflected in the way employees treat customers or clients. Interestingly, supervisors treat their subordinates the way they are treated by business owners.

- This exhortation becomes relevant: You don't need to convince people to buy from you. Rather treat your employees with the respect and the dignity they deserve and then they shall do the rest for you.

- The same is true for educational institutions. The way teachers and lecturers interact with learners or students can be linked to how stable and healthy their relationships are with their supervisors. As social beings, we tend to display what we get from one end by giving it to the other end.
- People don't care about what you know, what you do and what you have. They are more concerned with how you make them feel.
- Customers should not be privy to employees' frustrations because this will affect their relationship with the business. Remember, the notion of 'customers are always right'. This is important because it avoids what might affect the business, and it maintains healthy business-customer relationships.
- Spoil your employees or subordinates because they are pivotal and are the anchors that ensure your business or organisation is stable and survives.
- It is noble to yield. Recognising the role employees play in all that a business or organisation does is the beginning of successful leadership.
- As a leader, you have to study and understand the environment in which you operate. You have to know when people have had enough of your methods and, in turn, adjust and begin to sympathise and reason with them.
- Everyone involved in, or who is part of, a business or organisation is as important as everyone else.

To end, I am quite sure that you will begin to value your work more than you do your job (if you have one). While jobs may, at times, be frustrating and not necessarily offer you what you really want, your work is vitally important. It is your identity, and you should thus be encouraged to always do your best in your job or in any assignment you are given.

If you work for an organisation or business, be a team player, learn from those doing the most at work, and, where possible, motivate and embolden others to work – to work really hard. When serving, serve with passion and diligence, for there is satisfaction in looking back at your excellent achievements. As you continue to do well and move forward, be an asset, never a liability.

Find joy in your work; it is your pride and the image that markets you. Remember that when you do well, praise will always be about you and your accomplishments, and not about your job. May you be transformed by this book!

REFERENCES

Cleaver, A. 40 Reasons to Keep Studying. https://www.theodysseyonline.com/40-reasons-to-keep-studying.

Doby, D. The Value of Small Acts. https://jamesclear.com/3-2-1/june-30-2022.

Education- ASDEPO. https://asdepo.org/?page_id=63.

Fanon, F. (n.d.). *Theory of Cognitive Dissonance.* https://www.cram.com/essay/Frantz-Fanons-Theory-Of-Cognitive-Dissonance/F33ZTU9UR44X.

Kurtus, R. 2021. *Importance of Character in Your Career.* https://www.school-for-champions.com/career/importance_of_personal_character.ht.

The Holy Bible. 1995. New International Version. (Matthew 7:12). Bible Society of South Africa.

Munroe, M. 2007. *Releasing Your Potential: Exposing the Hidden You.*

Naziev, A. What Is An Education? International Conference: The Future of Education. https://conference.pixel-online.net/FOE/files/foe/ed0007/FP/3570-SOE2462-FP-   FOE7.pdf.

Ngombe, A.M. 2021. *Being Intelligently Emotional: Unlocking the power of Ubuntu in Africa for success in leadership and entrepreneurship.* Windhoek, Namibia.

Nikodemus, S, T. 2010. *Principles for the 21st Century Leader: Fly With The Eagle and Rise Beyond Mediocrity.* Windhoek: Truelead Training Institute.

Stanley, A. Leaders Who Don't Listen. https://www.linkedin.com/pulse/
must-read-leaders-who-   dont-listen-eventually-surrounded-alex-
kroon.

The Global Career Hub. *5 Reasons Why (and how) to Add Value to Your
Employer.* https://mycareer.aicpa-cima.com/article/5-reasons-why-
and-how-to-add-value-to-your-   employer

Winfrey, O. https://www.pinterest.com/pin/435371488956016850/.

Yeats, W, B. The Power of Education. https://www.facebook.com/
StadioNamibiaFormerlySBS/photos/a.621365728044100/197186814
9660511/?type=3.